MW00889444

This Notebook belongs to:

Made in United States
Troutdale, OR
11/29/2023

15119677R00069